PHILADELPHIA
THEN & NOW

PHILADELPHIA THEN & NOW

EDWARD ARTHUR MAUGER

ThunderBay
P·R·E·S·S

San Diego, California

Thunder Bay Press
An imprint of the Advantage Publishers Group
10350 Barnes Canyon Road, San Diego, CA 92121
www.thunderbaybooks.com

THUNDER BAY
P·R·E·S·S

Produced by Salamander Books,
an imprint of Anova Books Company Ltd.,
10 Southcombe Street, London, W14 0RA, United Kingdom

All notations of errors or omissions should be addressed to Thunder Bay Press, Editorial Department, at the above address. All other correspondence (author inquiries, permissions) concerning the content of this book should be addressed to Salamander Books, 10 Southcombe Street, London, W14 0RA, United Kingdom.

ISBN-13: 978-1-59223-864-4
ISBN-10: 1-59223-864-5

The Library of Congress has cataloged the original Thunder Bay edition as follows:

Mauger, Edward Arthur.
Philadelphia then and now / Edward Arthur Mauger.
p. cm.
ISBN 1-57145-880-8
1. Philadelphia (Pa.)--Pictorial works. 2. Philadelphia (Pa.)--History--Pictorial works. I. Title.

F158.37 .M46 2002
974.8'11'002--dc21

2002031955

Printed and bound in China

1 2 3 4 5 12 11 10 09 08

ACKNOWLEDGMENTS

Many thanks to these cordial guardians of Philadelphia's rich photographic legacy for their help: Erika Piola of the Library Company, Joseph Benford of the Philadelphia Free Library, and Margaret Jerrido of the Temple Urban Archives. Several modern photos were secured with the help of the Miller and Peyton Committee. One of Philadelphia's finest, Frank Margeson, chased down the light to obtain key color photographs. Of course, master photographer Simon Clay was at his intrepid best leaning from a helicopter, scrambling on rooftops, and slipping onto the grounds of a maximum security prison for the best photos of Philadelphia. The text benefited from Ron Avery's readiness to rein in the author's unbridled enthusiasm for Philadelphia with actual facts. More than anyone, Dr. Julianne Baird assisted the author with the project from start to finish. Whenever a phrase begins to sing, it was coaxed by Baird. Of the dozens of publications that have informed the text, two served regularly: *Philadelphia—A 300-Year History* edited by Russell F. Weigley and *Philadelphia Architecture* published by the Foundation for Architecture.

PHOTO CREDITS

The publisher wishes to thank the following for kindly providing the "then" photographs: 6, 10 (main and inset), 24, 38 (inset), 52, 60, 100, 114, 122, and 130 courtesy of the Library Company of Philadelphia; 8, 12, 20, 28, 36, 38 (main), 40 (main and inset), 42, 56, 62, 72, 76, 88, 96, 124 (main), 126, 138, and 140 courtesy of Urban Archives, Temple University Libraries; 14 courtesy of Amy Sarner Williams, the Clay Studio; 16, 18 (main and inset), 30, 32, 34, 48, 54, 58, 64, 66, 74, 82, 84, 86 (courtesy of Joseph Benfore), 94, 98, 116, and 134 courtesy of Castner Collection, Free Library of Philadelphia; 22 (main), 26, 44, 50, 68, 70, 78, 80, 90, 92, 102, 104, 106, 108, 110, 112, 118 (main and inset), 120, 124 (inset), 128, 132, 136, and 142 courtesy of City Archives, Philadelphia Department of Records; 22 (inset) courtesy of Arch Street Friends; 46 courtesy of Carol Smith, Philadelphia Contributionship.

Thanks to Frank Margeson for photographing the images from Temple University Libraries and the Philadelphia City Archives.

Thanks to Simon Clay for taking all the "now" photography in this book, with the exception of the photographs on the following pages: 9, 11, 31 (main), 35 (main), 67, 69, 85 (main), 87, 95, 123 (inset), and 131, photographer: Frank Margeson; 31 (inset) courtesy of the Pennsylvania Convention Center (photographer: Carol Highsmith); 63 courtesy of Lisa Bass, the Bourse; 113 (inset) courtesy of Philadelphia Museum of Art (photographer: © Nick Kelsh); 121 (inset) courtesy of Academy of Music.

Pages 1 and 2 show a view of Center City Philadelphia from the steps of the Museum of Art, then (photo: Urban Archives, Temple University Libraries) and now (photo: Simon Clay). See pages 42 and 43 for further details. For cover photo captions and credits, please see jacket.

INTRODUCTION

Philadelphia was a "London in wealth and more than a London in arrogance" when Colonel Washington arrived for the First Congress in 1774. Delegates from the other colonies were amazed at the handsome redbrick town houses lining the streets, the elegant churches, and taverns of every sort, one for every fifty men. What a contrast to the primitive village William Penn found when he arrived in 1682: Some English colonists were living in simple log huts, while others occupied the caves along the thirty-foot bank of the Delaware River. Even the tavern intended to greet Penn when his ship reached port remained unfinished.

The native Lenape were curious to meet this unusual Englishman who had already sent notice of his peaceful intentions. Although King Charles pressed Penn to take a regiment of soldiers for protection against "those savages," Penn objected. "The Indians . . . have been killed and robbed by the settlers. Let us now try what Love will do."

Determined to set "an example to the Nations," this radical Founding Father also changed the odds for the disenfranchised. Although most countries had official churches, Pennsylvania afforded "liberty of conscience." Penn saw democracy as a natural result of religious liberty—both based on trust in the common man—and established an elected assembly. Settlers seeking their fortunes hiked to the colony that was "heaven for farmers and artisans," but "hell for preachers and politicians."

One of these "strolling poor" arrived from Boston in 1723 with three pennies in his pocket and a disdain for overbearing authority; it did not take long for Benjamin Franklin's inventive spirit to find a home in Philadelphia. By 1774, Franklin and his associates had started America's first fire company, lending library, hospital, medical school, think tank, police force, paved streets, systematic street lighting, and insurance company. Franklin's success in publishing and in managing the postal service made Philadelphia the nerve center of colonial communications.

When Thomas Jefferson arrived in 1775 for the Second Congress, his keen architectural eye saw a city more beautiful than Paris. He took full advantage of Philadelphia's amenities. After he voted on his famous "Declaration" at the Statehouse on July 4, 1776, he walked a block north to America's best market and purchased fourteen pairs of ladies gloves. Philadelphia would serve as Jefferson's second home until the new nation's capital shifted in 1800.

As the country burgeoned in the nineteenth century, Philadelphia's leadership in science and the arts earned it the title "Athens of America"— it had the first art school and a museum, the first musicians' organization and first music publisher, and the Chestnut Street and Walnut Street theaters. Benjamin Franklin's primacy in the eighteenth-century print world blossomed into the nation's leading publishing houses. His scientific associations generated many nineteenth-century initiatives, including the first publications and professional organizations in medicine, psychiatry, chemistry, ornithology, botany, and architecture, and the world's first school of pharmacy. Philadelphia inventor John Fitch demonstrated the first working steamboat to delegates at the Constitutional Convention in 1787. Two decades later, Thomas Leiper's wooden railway tracks running from the Delaware River spawned another new industry in Philadelphia that reached its apex in the Baldwin Locomotive Works, the world's largest. Philadelphia was the manufacturing center for steamships, streetcars, locomotives, textiles, cigars, and hats—the famous Stetson cowboy hat was made here.

Philadelphia's architectural leadership included several of America's landmark Greek Revival buildings, the First and Second Banks and the Merchants Exchange. The Athenaeum, built on Sixth Street in 1845, spawned the Renaissance Revival style throughout the city and country. By the late nineteenth century, Philadelphia's Center City streetscape was dominated by large-scale Victorian and Renaissance Revival buildings and crowned by the world's largest masonry structure, City Hall. The stunning interior public spaces of buildings like the Bourse and Wanamaker's were matched by great outdoor spaces. The Waterworks became one of America's top nineteenth-century tourist attractions; people promenaded among its Roman temples and gardens. The world's largest city park, Fairmount, boasted America's first zoo and a cemetery so finely landscaped that visitors were limited by a ticket system.

While the Victorian-era city grew to full flower, Philadelphia's colonial neighborhoods gradually deteriorated. Houses in Old City were converted to shops or replaced by warehouses. Society Hill became a haven for immigrants who crowded into the town houses, seeking their footing in a new land. It was not until the 1950s that these architectural gems were rediscovered and restored.

Philadelphia's twentieth-century development was vertically restrained, as new buildings were held to the height of William Penn's statue on top of City Hall. Once the height limit was lifted in the 1990s, the city experienced a growth spurt of skyscrapers. The city's most dazzling new feature is the 150-foot-high glass arch crowning the Kimmel Center for the Performing Arts.

Unsurpassed in America in Victorian architecture, Parisian style, and Georgian buildings, boasting more public art than any other city in the world, Philadelphia has attracted more urban residents than almost any other American city. What makes Philadelphia unique among all the great cities is its colonial heritage—the most significant decisions of the eighteenth-century world were made in Philadelphia.

At the dedication of the world's longest suspension bridge on July 1, 1926, the governor of Pennsylvania proclaimed: "Blessed be the tie that binds." Ironically, one tie never connected was the track from the Philadelphia subway to the bridge. The governor, feuding with the mayor of Philadelphia, refused to link the tracks to those already laid across the bridge from Camden, New Jersey. As a result, four subway stations sit unused inside architect Paul Cret's massive stone towers. The station's colorful tiles depict advances in transportation through the centuries, up to the invention of the airship, or dirigible.

Besides modernizing the roadbed and painting the bridge blue, the greatest change since the bridge's opening is in the price of the toll: in 1926, pedestrians leading their horses paid twenty cents, men on horseback fifteen cents, and cars twenty-five cents—now it's three dollars (westbound only). Another significant change, which shows up only at night, is the spotlights that illuminate the suspenders and cast a gentle glow on the bridge's graceful arc. In both photographs, the bridge frames Center City Philadelphia.

ST. GEORGE'S CHURCH

Left: The world's oldest Methodist church in continuous use began as a German Reformed meetinghouse in 1767. Construction debts landed the trustees in jail and the building was auctioned off. The winning bid was $700—from a young boy. When he went home and told his dad that he had just bought a church, the distraught father tried to void the sale. The auctioneer refused, unless the man would declare his son mentally unfit. Instead, the man sold the building at a $50 loss to the Methodists in 1769.

Right: Construction of the Benjamin Franklin Bridge originally threatened the church with demolition in 1921, but a national protest led by retired Bishop Thomas B. Neely forced the bridge commission to reroute the Philadelphia side of the bridge so it would bypass St. George's by fourteen feet. To accommodate the excavation of Fourth Street, which was lowered to fit under the bridge, a new basement and retaining wall were added to the church.

Left: Did the woman who sewed the first American flag live here? This 1859 photograph shows identical town houses: a bakery on the left and cigar store on the right. Thirty years later, the bakery was gone (*see inset*). In 1895, Charles Weisgerber, who had immortalized Betsy Ross in his life-sized painting at the 1893 World's Fair, led a campaign to save the remaining house from demolition. One million children purchased ten-cent certificates to save the Betsy Ross House.

Right: Now millions of children visit this house to honor one of the few women ranked in the revolutionary pantheon. Ironically, they may be visiting the wrong house in search of a different kind of woman than the one they imagine. Not quite the sweet matronly seamstress painted by Weisgerber, Betsy was a fiercely independent twentysomething spitfire during the Revolution. Some historians argue that she probably lived in the house that was torn down.

William Penn viewed cramped alleys such as Elfreth's as an affront to his plans for a "green countrie towne," with lush gardens on two-acre plots. Yet, as a miniature melting pot, it fulfilled the most radical part of his vision. Mary Smith ran her own dressmaking shop at 126 Elfreth's Alley; Moses Mordicai, founding member of the city's first synagogue, lived in 118; and Cuff Douglas, a free black tailor, in 117. The Quaker shipwright in 124 supplied boats to evacuate Washington's wounded soldiers from the Brandywine battlefield in 1777.

Elfreth's Alley, America's oldest residential street, has celebrated its three hundredth birthday. No longer a haven for the "lower sorts," this charming street is lined with restored town houses. Its proud residents have their own association to welcome the thousands of tourists who visit this popular site. Two of the houses are open daily to the public for a nominal fee.

Philadelphia's Old City has seen three centuries of change. Many of the shops and warehouses that had flourished in the nineteenth century were standing vacant by the 1950s, including these buildings, which were photographed a little later. Two centuries earlier, Old City was a neighborhood of working-class town houses for people like Betsy Ross and Jeremiah Elfreth. One section was crowded with poorhouses and rowdy taverns, including the Three Jolly Irishmen, where Cock Robin and his two wives engaged in gambling, drugs, and prostitution. Even Washington's own servants slipped out to carouse in "Helltown."

In the 1960s, struggling artists gravitated to Old City's low-cost industrial buildings. Their large sunlit interiors were well suited for lofts. Founded in 1974, the Clay Studio renovated these adjoining buildings and became one of the first successful artists' cooperatives in the area. It sparked an influx of studios and design firms, which now host Philadelphia's renowned "First Friday." Once a month, more than fifty galleries in Old City open their doors for an evening of art, music, and street theater.

America's first stock market was organized in 1754 in the London Coffee House at Front and Market streets. Some merchants frequented the taverns, but many realized that the brew in the coffeehouses kept them more alert for their business deals. Wives objected that the men slighted their domestic duties to spend all day in the coffeehouses.

The London Coffee House was surpassed in the 1770s by the City Tavern, located one block over—the "most genteel in the colonies," according to John Adams. Even George Washington dabbled in stocks at the City Tavern. The London Coffee House was later converted into a tobacco and segar (cigar) store and finally demolished. A late-nineteenth-century brick building now sits vacant on this corner, a sad replacement for the robust colonial trading center.

In 1681, William Penn's city plan gave High Street, Philadelphia's main east-west street, a width of one hundred feet. Very soon a market developed, in the European custom, down the middle of the street. Two decades later, the market shed stretched for four blocks, with a two-story head house near the Delaware River. On market days, Wednesdays and Saturdays, the Pennsylvania farmers hauled their produce into town in Conestoga, or covered, wagons, an invention of Penn's erudite secretary, James Logan.

The 1859 photograph shows an ornate cupola crowning the market on the site of the original colonial head house. High Street has been renamed Market Street. By the twentieth century, the market sheds had been demolished to lay trolley tracks. In the inset photo from circa 1905 (*opposite*), the trolleys roll down the middle of Market and turn around at the east end. The bus passenger shelter designed like a market shed is the only current reminder of the great Philadelphia market.

The facade of the Smythe Building is a fine example of Northern Italian Renaissance style. Its graceful arched windows allow much more natural light than those in masonry buildings. Until the Industrial Revolution, a "prefab" cast-iron building like the Smythe was not practical. It required a modern nineteenth-century foundry to produce these connecting metal sections. Without railroads to transport the heavy pieces, their manufacture would not have been cost-effective.

The original photo (*opposite*) shows only the right side of the building because the central portion was completely removed in 1913 to accommodate a trolley turnaround. To restore the building in 1984, the center section of the facade was rebuilt using fiberglass molded from the remaining cast-iron sections. The restored Smythe Building is now a successful apartment complex.

William Penn's Quakers thrived in Pennsylvania. In the early 1800s, their numbers justified building this large meetinghouse (*see inset*). Here women were initiated into leadership roles, creating schools, establishing charities, and resolving disputes. Lucretia Mott, clerk of the women's business meeting, was reputed to have organized the Underground Railroad to help slaves reach freedom once they had crossed the Mason-Dixon Line into Pennsylvania. These women later led the campaign to give women the right to vote.

The Arch Street building, the largest Quaker meetinghouse in the world, maintains its plain style, including clear glass windows, white walls, no steeple, and simple benches. The Friends are still opposed to "hireling clergy," and their hallmark remains active participation by all members. Even Sunday worship services rely on the spontaneous testimony of the members. Although the Sunday congregation is much reduced from its nineteenth-century numbers, the building is open to a steady stream of guests and tourists on weekdays.

David Rittenhouse, colonial clockmaker and amateur astronomer, built his grand home on the corner of Seventh and Mulberry streets, the same spot where he often set up his telescope. Among the accomplishments that brought him renown in both the colonies and Europe, Rittenhouse recalculated the distance from the earth to the moon. He was a member of Ben Franklin's American Philosophical Society, succeeding him as president of the group. This 1859 photo shows his mansion.

Mulberry—later renamed Arch Street because of the bridge erected at the Delaware River end to span a thirty-foot drop—eventually became a commercial strip. African Americans, whose ancestors followed the stars in the night sky to find their way to freedom, now celebrate their history and culture where Rittenhouse once traced the heavens. The African American Museum in Philadelphia, a Bicentennial project, was one of the first such museums in America.

The PSFS building, seen from City Hall's tower, was America's first International Style skyscraper. George Howe and Swiss architect William Lescaze introduced this strikingly modern structure into Philadelphia's streetscape in 1932. The huge illuminated letters on the roof of the Philadelphia Saving Fund Society building are an integral part of the design. Even though the building was constructed during the Depression, no expense was spared: clocks, fixtures, and even the furniture were custom designed by the architects. It was one of the first buildings to have air-conditioning.

The Philadelphia Saving Fund Society, founded in 1816, was the first savings bank in America. In 1992 it was bought out by another bank, which subsequently folded. Loews purchased and converted the building into a luxury hotel, preserving many of its original features. The PSFS sign still lights up the Philadelphia night sky, sharing the limelight with the Aramark sign atop its modern headquarters across Market Street.

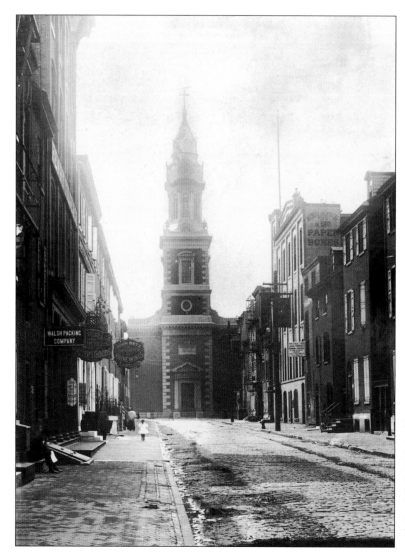

In 1796, President George Washington, an Episcopalian, donated $50 toward the construction of a Catholic church for the Brothers of the Order of Hermits of St. Augustine. The original structure was destroyed by fire in 1844, and the present building was designed by famed architect Napoleon Le Brun. Its interior is rich with Italian frescoes. Villanova, the first Roman Catholic college in Pennsylvania, was also founded on this site.

St. Augustine's has been host to great music making, including the American premieres of Handel's *Messiah*, Haydn's *Creation*, and Rossini's *Little Solemn Mass*. The Choral Society and Orchestra established by organist Henry Gordon eventually grew into the world-renowned Philadelphia Orchestra. The church's grand entrance was "lowered" in the 1920s when Fourth Street was excavated for the Benjamin Franklin Bridge. The outline of the original doorway can be seen on the brick face in the modern photograph.

Left: In 1893, the Reading Railroad Terminal replaced the farmers' and butchers' markets on the same site. These two buildings had themselves been mid-nineteenth-century replacements for the original colonial market. That market was an open-air pavilion that extended up the middle of the street from the Delaware River past Washington's executive mansion at Sixth Street. Moving the market indoors improved sanitation and opened up the street for trolley tracks.

Right: The Head House of the Reading Terminal is a graceful Italian Renaissance building that housed offices and a passenger station until 1984. The train shed, which spread behind it for two city blocks, features the world's largest steel span arch. This landmark has been preserved as a grand entrance and ballroom for the Pennsylvania Convention Center (inset shows the interior of the building). America's oldest farmers' market still operates at street level under the shed, attracting residents and restaurant chefs alike. Office workers and conventioneers have their pick of eateries, from Asian to Mexican to Amish.

The Lit family's clothing store had become so successful that in 1895 the family began buying up buildings along the entire block of Market Street, from Seventh to Eighth. This 1898 photograph shows Lit Brothers with the Eighth Street half of their expansion finished. By 1907, they had added large buildings at both corners, complete with octagonal towers. All of the sections were in Renaissance Revival style to match the original buildings.

Although the Lit Brothers store closed in 1977, it was saved from demolition. The interior has been turned into offices, with retail space on the lower floors. To preserve the only complete commercial block of Victorian architecture in Philadelphia, the exterior has been carefully restored. While its uniform color makes the building look like it is a single cast-iron structure, only one of the original eleven buildings, added by the Lit Brothers to join its fabulous facade, is actually cast iron.

Left: In 1875, John Wanamaker founded one of America's first department stores when he expanded his menswear shop and moved into a huge converted freight depot at Twelfth and Market streets. He immediately constructed a 10,200-seat auditorium in the building to host the religious crusaders Moody and Sankey. They preached to a million people, including President Grant, over a two-month period. After they moved on, Wanamaker hosted weekly events for the edification of the public.

Above: Starting in 1902, Wanamaker built his new store on that site in three separate stages, so that he could continue to sell. When the building was finished in 1911, it contained two million square feet of floor space—more than any other building at the time. The Wanamaker building has a five-story central court, featuring the world's largest pipe organ (*see inset*). The old department store is now defunct, but the public is still treated to free daily concerts.

Left: Edgar Allan Poe arrived in Philadelphia in 1837, hoping for success in America's publishing empire. The house at Seventh and Spring Garden was apparently the inspiration for one of his first mysteries, *The Black Cat*. Visitors can still see the bricked-in area in the basement that inspired Poe to have his protagonist inter his wife and one-eyed cat.

Above: Poe's famous poem "The Raven" was inspired by a Charles Dickens novel that featured his own pet raven, Grip, as a talking bird. The Dickens/Poe raven, now stuffed, is perched in the Rare Book Room of the Philadelphia Free Library. Poe's Seventh Street house is maintained by the National Park Service and is open to the public. What is now the rear wing of the building was actually the apartment used by Poe and his family.

In June 1776, Thomas Jefferson moved from the noisy, bustling heart of colonial Philadelphia to the outskirts—Seventh and Market streets. There, in rooms rented from Jacob Graff, he could concentrate on writing the explanation America would provide for severing ties with England. Like the other Founding Fathers, he was destined to spend half his public career within three blocks of Independence Hall.

The mid-nineteenth-century photo shows the Graff House as a printing office and store, part of Market Street's busy commercial strip. Torn down in 1883, the Graff House was replaced by a flamboyant Gothic Revival–style bank building designed by Frank Furness (*see inset, opposite*). The site is now occupied by a replica of the Graff House, Declaration House, built by the National Park Service in honor of Jefferson's document.

Sunday after Sunday during the 1790s, six matching bay horses would draw a grand white coach up to Christ Church, and President and Mrs. Washington would alight and join the congregation. Although Deborah Franklin had insisted that they rent a family pew, Ben's own attendance was sporadic. He is now permanently interred in the Franklin family plot at Christ Church's Fifth Street cemetery, near more signers of the Declaration and Constitution than are buried anywhere else in America. The inset shows the interior of the church.

Christ Church is among America's most elegant buildings. The long walls feature sculpted brick, graceful rows of arched windows like a Roman aqueduct, and exuberant balustrades with carved tongues of flame. The eastern wall boasts a majestic Palladian window (*see inset*). Ben Franklin raised the funds for the steeple; he needed a promontory to test his theories on electricity and lightning. The 204-foot tower made Christ Church the tallest building in eighteenth-century America. They say ship's captains still look for this landmark as they sail up the Delaware River.

The view of Center City from the steps of the Philadelphia Museum of Art is perhaps the city's most famous vista. Inspired by the popular *Rocky* movies, hundreds of visitors charge up the museum steps daily and turn in triumph toward downtown Philadelphia. This early photograph shows the new Benjamin Franklin Parkway in the 1930s, its trees in adolescent growth. The tallest building in Philadelphia has no rivals, as nothing was permitted to top the statue of William Penn perched on the City Hall tower.

The modern photograph shows a transformed skyline after One Liberty Place (with the spire, at right) rose nearly one thousand feet in 1987. It now has the company of other skyscrapers clustered around it. The heroic statue of Washington (in the foreground) is one of America's first great monuments to the military leader. Ironically, he gazes up the Parkway to City Hall and the statue of Penn, the pacifist founder of Pennsylvania—two wise founders with noble but different visions.

Benjamin Franklin founded the American Philosophical Society in 1743 for "the promoting of Useful Knowledge" in medicine, science, brewing, and any improvement in "the Power of Man over Matter." Its home was established at Philosophical Hall in 1789. Some of the first members of America's first think tank assisted Franklin in his electrical experiments. Those elected to the society include Thomas Jefferson, its third president; James Madison; Albert Einstein; Charles Darwin; and Marie Curie.

The 1929 photograph (*opposite*) shows Philosophical Hall with an added third floor to hold its distinguished document collection. In 1949 this addition—which was deemed discordant with its surroundings—was removed, requiring a special act of Congress, since the building is now on national park land, next to Independence Hall.

The Philadelphia Contributionship was founded in 1752 by Benjamin Franklin. The Great Fire of London was on the minds of Philadelphia's founders when they used brick for their houses and forebade smoking on the streets. In 1781, the Contributionship announced that trees were a fire hazard and had to be eliminated. The Greentree, a rival insurance company, was quickly organized to let people keep their sylvan surroundings, but for a higher fee.

The Philadelphia Contributionship, now America's oldest continuously operating corporation, remains at its Fourth Street site. Its current building was designed in 1836 by Thomas U. Walter, who won fame for his work on the U.S. Capitol. Like its neoclassic neighbors throughout Society Hill, the Contributionship is constructed of Philadelphia's famous red brick; it is distinguished by its elegant French features, paired columns, paired windows, and a mansard roof.

Philadelphia's best Federal-style house was built in 1786 for Henry Hill, a wine merchant. He became rich importing Madeira, the only wine that actually improved when it crossed the Atlantic. Dr. Philip Syng Physick moved into the house in 1815 with his four children. His wife, with one of America's first prenuptial agreements, apparently divorced him for cutting down her favorite tree.

Grandson of the silversmith who made the inkstands at Independence Hall, Physick used his skillful hands to earn the title "Father of American Surgery." His home has been elegantly restored by the Philadelphia Society for the Preservation of Landmarks and is open as a museum. Tours of the house include a room displaying Dr. Physick's medical instruments. Some of his inventions remain in use today, including forceps, the curved needle, and soda pop.

America's first hospital, established through Ben Franklin's efforts in 1756, put Philadelphia on the cutting edge of colonial medicine. Jefferson brought his daughter to Philadelphia for vaccination against the dreaded smallpox, since the Virginia Assembly had banned such an "intrusion against nature." Dr. Benjamin Rush, the "Father of American Psychiatry," attended the insane housed in the hospital; he had studied mental illness scientifically and devised forms of occupational therapy.

The original Eighth Street building was dramatically enlarged in 1804 with a center pavilion and a matching west wing. The top floor of the pavilion houses the world's oldest operating room, now restored and open to the public. There, visitors can see where the renowned Dr. Physick once operated under the gaze of the medical students in the first gallery, with the paying public in the upper gallery.

Left: In the 1800s, the exodus of Philadelphia residents from this first colonial neighborhood near the Delaware River left it open for the development of warehouses and shops. This 1876 photograph shows the first Corn Exchange building at the corner of Second and Chestnut. Inside was a wholesale exchange and bank for merchants trading in grains, groceries, and woolens.

Above: In 1900, the Corn Exchange corporation decided to construct a new building on the corner, in Colonial Revival style. However, to reflect the Corn Exchange's new status as one of Philadelphia's wealthiest banks, the architect transformed this normally unassuming design into a grand rococo building. It is festooned with elaborate pediments above the doors, carved wreaths and swags around the windows, and an ornate clock tower on the corner. The Corn Exchange still contains a bank, as well as a newspaper office and restaurants.

The colonial delegates to the First Continental Congress sweltered through the hot 1774 autumn in Carpenters' Hall. They chose this private building to foil the British spies. Here Patrick Henry unfurled his impressive oratory: "I am not a Virginian, but an American." At the time, Ben Franklin's lending library—America's first—was stored upstairs. There Franklin had a crucial meeting with an agent of the French crown to secure the secret trade agreement required if the colonies should decide on independence.

Carpenters' Hall is still the guild hall for America's oldest trade organization, the Worshipful Carpenters Company of Philadelphia, founded in 1724. The building, designed by Robert Smith, was completed in 1774. After the Revolution, various organizations rented the hall until they could move into their own quarters. The First Bank, the Musical Fund Society, and the College of Pharmacy all started there. In the mid-nineteenth century, it was also used as an auction house.

Built on the oldest plot of land owned by African Americans, this is the founding church for all African Methodist Episcopal churches, now in six different nations. The first African Methodist Episcopal church building was a blacksmith's shop hauled to the site in 1794. The Reverend Richard Allen, America's first black minister, "licensed to exhort," established this first independent African American church after encountering hostility in St. George's Methodist Church.

Mother Bethel Church was an important stop on the Underground Railroad and hosted many abolitionist leaders, including Lucretia Mott and Frederick Douglass. When the current building was completed in 1890, Philadelphia had a large middle-class African American population. This structure, the fourth on the site, was designed in the very grand Richardson Romanesque style of Victorian-era architecture. Mother Bethel welcomes visitors from around the world to its active church and historic museum.

Left: Congress refused to renew the charter for the First National Bank in 1811, leaving the United States unprepared for war with England in 1812. The Second Bank was organized to fill the financial gap. Insisting on the "Greek style," Nicholas Biddle held a design contest for the building. The winner was Philadelphian William Strickland. Completed in 1824, the Second Bank became the architectural prototype for America's banks. People felt their money was safe in a such a grand classical building.

Above: Populist President Jackson, suspicious of the federal bank's power, withdrew government funds and distributed them to his favorite state banks. The Second Bank closed in 1834. The building served as the Federal Customs House until 1934. Now it houses an exhibition of Charles Willson Peale's paintings of the Founding Fathers and Mothers. The National Park Service conducts tours of the collection.

This early photograph shows the 1790 building of the Library Company. Benjamin Franklin and his community-minded colleagues actually started the library in 1731, paying forty shillings apiece. Franklin later noted the political implications for America: "Libraries made the common Tradesman as intelligent as most Gentlemen . . . and contributed to the Stand the Colonies made in Defense of their Privileges."

This modern photograph shows a duplicate building constructed on the site to house the library of Franklin's American Philosophical Society. This distinguished library includes a copy of the Declaration of Independence in Thomas Jefferson's own hand and Benjamin Franklin's copy of the Constitution. As with the original building, a statue of Ben Franklin in a toga stands in the niche over the front door. The Founding Fathers began to see themselves as heirs to the great republics of Greece and Rome.

BOURSE BUILDING

Built in 1895, the Bourse was America's first commodities exchange. This block-long building accommodated a variety of financial institutions, including the Maritime Exchange and Stock Exchange, as well as grain-trading activities. It was one of the first buildings in Philadelphia to be constructed of steel framing. After the financial district shifted toward the center of Philadelphia, the Bourse fell into decline. By the mid-twentieth century, it was a down-at-the-heels auction house and warehouse.

The Bourse building was renovated in 1982 to create a three-tiered open retail mall and modern offices. Restored to its original Victorian splendor of polished brass balconies and ornate plasterwork, the interior court is one of Philadelphia's great spaces (*see inset*). Located directly across Fifth Street from Independence National Historical Park, it is now a convenient mix of shops, eateries, and services. The gorgeous sandstone, Pompeian brick, and terra-cotta exterior has been faithfully restored to its original splendor.

The First Presbyterian Church decided to sponsor a new building on Pine Street for the residents of Society Hill in 1766. Insisting that the minister adhere to the "Old Order," they chose Samuel Eakin, newly married and just graduated from Princeton Seminary. The Eakins had their first child six months later and Samuel was ousted for "antenuptial fornication." Over the objections of the First Church, the congregation then chose a "New Light" minister, George Duffield, a fiery preacher who eventually led his congregants into the Revolutionary army.

Today, Old Pine Street is America's oldest Presbyterian church. Used as a hospital for the British troops during their occupation of the city and then as a stable, it presented a sad spectacle for Duffield upon his return from the war. President Adams rented a pew here, observing that the sermons "more nearly resemble those of our New England Clergy." The congregation "modernized" the simple colonial building in the nineteenth century, raising the roof and adding Corinthian columns.

This 1855 photograph shows a bookseller's stall attached to America's oldest congressional building. During its first decade, Congress cut its legislative teeth here, creating the Bill of Rights, the first new states, the first census, and the reapportionment of delegates. A bristling President Washington, insisting on his presidential prerogatives, dared Congress to impeach him in their pursuit of his secret correspondence regarding the treaty with England.

To the left of Congress Hall is the Pennsylvania Statehouse, which Lafayette dubbed the "Hall of Independence" upon his return in 1824. One of America's best Georgian buildings, Independence Hall was designed by Philadelphia lawyer Andrew Hamilton. In fact, it was his triumph in the celebrated Zenger case that earned shrewd lawyers the nickname "Philadelphia lawyer." These buildings, where the most critical political debates of the eighteenth century still echo, have been faithfully restored and are open daily to visitors.

Left: London? Dublin? No, Philadelphia is where theater buffs must look for the oldest continuously used English-speaking theater in the world. A theatrical who's who has trod the boards, including Sarah Bernhardt, George M. Cohan, Claudette Colbert, Harry Houdini, Helen Hayes, Groucho Marx, and Katharine Hepburn. America's two great theatrical dynasties, both from Philadelphia, the Forrest/Booth family and the Barrymores, were frequent performers at the Walnut Street Theatre.

Above: Built in 1809, the Walnut Street Theatre was renovated in 1828 with a Greek Revival facade by architect John Haviland. After years of accretions, the building was restored in 1972 to its Haviland exterior and the interior was fully modernized. Today, the Walnut Street Theatre presents one of the most successful regional series in the country.

South Street has always been Philadelphia's Bohemian strip. Originally named Cedar, it marked the southern edge of the city. Since Quakers viewed theater as "a waste of God's time," the theaters were built south of the city limits; colonial Philadelphians had to skip town for such sinful pursuits. When the British army occupied the city in 1778, Major Andre used his time painting sets for productions to amuse his fellow officers at the theaters on the other side of South Street.

South Street was a neighborhood for Jewish immigrants in the 1930s, and its shops sold everything from groceries to fine furs. In the 1950s a failed scheme to turn the street into a crosstown expressway left many stores vacant. Today ethnic eateries such as Alyan's, Mirchi, and Mallorca mix with stores such as the Mad Hatter, Zipperhead, and Condom Kingdom. It's a great place to eat, shop, people-watch, or have something pierced or tattooed.

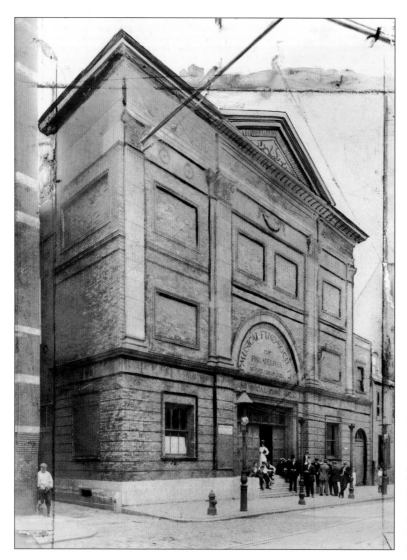

America's first professional music organization built the Musical Fund Hall in 1824 to house a recital hall and provide for the "relief of decayed musicians." The "Swedish Nightingale," Jenny Lind, and novelists Thackeray and Dickens appeared here. The world's first regular medical college for women held its commencement here in 1851. Women who tried to break into this "manly" profession were warned that they would exhibit symptoms of "monstrous brains and puny bodies; weak digestion; flowing thought and constipated bowels."

The Musical Fund Hall served as Philadelphia's primary concert space until 1857, when the Academy of Music was built on Broad Street. The hall gradually deteriorated during the twentieth century and has recently been converted into an apartment house.

Constructed between 1698 and 1699, Old Swedes (Gloria Dei Church) is the oldest church building in Pennsylvania. The congregation was descended from the colonists who sailed up the Delaware under the leadership of Governor Johan Prinz in 1643. Although the Swedes brought log construction to America, they decided to hire English masons and build their church out of brick.

The most notable Swedish pastor of Gloria Dei was Nils Collin, a friend of Ben Franklin's. Attempts to tame lightning were considered a challenge to Divine Providence, but Collin had Franklin's lightning rods installed on the building. Vestiges of those first lightning rods remain on Old Swedes, a National Historic Site.

Early Philadelphia had a strong French connection. The French loved Ben Franklin, and their political theorists admired Pennsylvania's egalitarian constitution. Even Joseph Bonaparte was welcomed to the city after his brother's defeat at Waterloo. The "good" Bonaparte settled in with the other two thousand French who had migrated to Philadelphia after their revolution went sour. Michael Bouvier, great-grandfather to Jacqueline, worked as a carpenter on Bonaparte's Ninth Street Estate.

The Bonaparte house is a private residence today. Occasionally a ghost tour will pass by the house relating the sad tale of Chloris Inglesby. Chloris, a dancer at a seedy tavern, and Bonaparte's aide became lovers. Chloris was shocked to find that he was due to sail back to Corsica to marry another woman. She stowed onboard the French ship in the harbor, resolved to change his mind once they were out to sea. Discovered before the ship cleared the harbor, she was confined in a small outbuilding on the Bonaparte property.

Left: John Todd died in the devastating yellow fever epidemic that killed five thousand city residents in 1793. After the scourge had passed, his wife, Dolley, moved back to their home at Fourth and Walnut. She at first "set her cap" for Senator Aaron Burr, who rented an upstairs apartment, but his colleague from Virginia, a brilliant little man with a large head, turned out to be a better prospect. It is said that James Madison and Dolley had their first "blind date" over tea in the second-floor front parlor.

Above: The archival photograph shows the house's previous twentieth-century life as a luncheonette. Perhaps Dolley Madison ice cream was served there for dessert, which is fitting since she introduced ice cream to the White House for husband James Madison's second inaugural ball. Now the Todd House is restored and open to the public for scheduled tours by the National Park Service.

One of the four members in President George Washington's cabinet, Treasurer Alexander Hamilton built up a Federal bureaucracy of three hundred employees on Third Street. As a leading proponent of big government, he hired more staff than the other three cabinet members combined. Hamilton understood the role of money better than the other founders: "Power without revenue is only a name." The first national bank became the centerpiece of his monetary program.

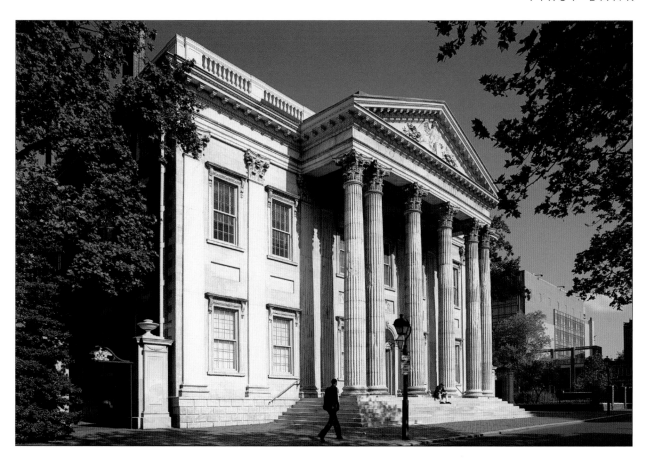

The National Park Service now uses the First Bank for offices and
storage. Completed in 1795, it was one of America's first Classical
Revival buildings, with marble-clad walls and Corinthian columns.
The American eagle over the portico is carved from mahogany but
painted to look like stone.

In a city of rectangular grids, William Strickland was faced with the problem of fitting America's oldest stock market on a triangular parcel of land. His graceful semicircular Greek Revival portico was the solution. The building was completed in 1833 and served as a stock exchange until the Civil War.

In the nineteenth century, the building became the focus for Philadelphia's wholesale food markets. Produce sheds surrounded the building. Once a modern distribution center was built in South Philadelphia, the sheds were torn down to reveal once more this exquisite classical building. The National Park Service recently renovated the building, which now serves as the headquarters for Independence National Historical Park.

St. Peter's, Philadelphia's second Anglican (Episcopal) church, is a celebration of colonial art and architecture. Robert Smith, who designed Carpenters' Hall, built the church in 1761. America's third great architect, William Strickland, added the tower in 1842. The statues *Praise* and *Exhortation* on the organ case were carved by America's first sculptor, William Rush. Charles Willson Peale, who founded the first art school and museum in America, is buried in the churchyard.

Peale has fascinating company in the churchyard—now obscured by the full-grown trees that were just saplings in the photo opposite—including eight Native American chiefs who contracted smallpox when they arrived to sign a peace treaty with President Washington in 1793; George Mifflin Dallas, whose name graces that Texas city; and Commodore Stephen Decatur, otherwise known as the "Shores of Tripoli" marine. Visitors can feel the power of the Revolution in box pew 41, the original bench occupied by President Washington.

In 1814, several young professionals formed a literary club to celebrate the classics, American history, and, in the spirit of Ben Franklin's American Philosophical Society, "the useful arts." The Athenaeum building, designed by John Notman in 1845, is America's first Renaissance Revival building. It started an architectural trend that swept through Philadelphia, and then across the nation. The relatively plain brownstone exterior is dramatized by a large overhanging cornice and deep-set crowns over the second-floor windows.

Named for the goddess of wisdom and learning, the Athenaeum
now houses one of the finest collections of architectural drawings and
photographs in the nation—from colonial master builders like Robert
Smith to modern architects like Robert Venturi. Although a member-
supported library, the Athenaeum is accessible to the public, as is its
extensive computer archive.

Left: The four-story town house in the center of this photo was built in 1759 for a pirate. Captain Abercrombie made a killing as a privateer for the English side of the French and Indian War. He was able to build the most grand Georgian town house in Philadelphia on Second Street with a view of the busy harbor. At the time of the photograph, the house was serving as a warehouse in the slums of Society Hill.

Above: A present-day photograph shows the Abercrombie House restored as a private dwelling. Its new neighbors are the Society Hill Towers, designed by internationally renowned architect I. M. Pei in 1964. Constructing the three modern apartment buildings was part of a successful strategy to attract middle-class residents back to a dilapidated section of Philadelphia. Society Hill is now one of the most desirable city neighborhoods in America.

The plain Quaker-built facade of this fine town house belies its lavish interior. When Samuel Powel purchased the house for his bride, Elizabeth, in 1769, he had the interior remodeled in a lavish high Georgian style. Their good friends George and Martha Washington duplicated features they admired at the Powel House in their Mount Vernon home. The general took time from the war to dance in the Powels' ballroom at his twentieth wedding anniversary in 1779.

The Powel House deteriorated with the rest
of Society Hill in the nineteenth century. The
ballroom where the Founding Fathers celebrated
had become part of a hogs-hair and horsehair
factory, producing brooms and ladies' corsets.
In the 1930s the indomitable Mrs. Wister and her
society friends purchased the house to save it from
demolition. Exquisitely restored and full of fine
eighteenth-century furnishings, many from the
Powel family, the house is now open to the public.

Brick mason John Drinker owned a narrow strip of land from Pine Street through to Delancey. He built his family home on Pine and these two small town houses on Delancey with a courtyard through to his back door. Since he had to pay taxes only on street frontage, he could clear a tidy profit renting each room on the inner court to a sailor or whole family. Because of the tax structure, colonial Philadelphia was full of these courtyards.

Society Hill took its name from the Free Society of Traders, the investment company originally set up by William Penn. Bankruptcy made their land available for the colonial city's expanding population. Society Hill plunged economically in the 1800s, becoming a haven for Jewish immigrants fleeing Russia and Eastern Europe. Declared a National Historic Neighborhood, Society Hill is the largest enclave of Georgian architecture in America.

The king of France once lived at Fourth and Prune. Louis-Philippe shared the house, now demolished, with his brother in 1797 before returning to take the French throne. The house on the south corner was home to Dr. William Shippen, who was in charge of medical care for the Revolutionary army. In 1798, Dr. Caspar Wistar moved in. Before embarking on the Lewis and Clark expedition, Meriweather Lewis studied with Wistar. The plant wisteria was named in his honor.

Farther south on the block is Olde St. Mary's Church. Town houses originally lined the street in front of the church: though Penn's constitution afforded freedom of religion, Catholics at first hid their churches from view. Adams and Washington attended a "Romish Mass" here in 1775. After participation in the Revolution, the Catholics tore down the houses and built their church out to the street. In contrast to the original Palladian style of church, the present facade is neo-Gothic, a more Roman Catholic style of architecture.

Left: Newmarket was built in 1745 to accommodate the new residents of Society Hill. Everybody came out on market days, especially if a hanging or other special event was scheduled. Some came more to "window shop" and gossip than to purchase goods, often crowding the aisles around the rented booths—a problem aggravated by the hoopskirts worn by ladies in the nineteenth century. The increasingly frustrated Pennsylvania farmers devised their own solution to break the gridlock: they would let frogs loose in the aisle, the ladies would scatter, and the farmers could then proceed with their sales.

Right: Today, Newmarket is restored and serves as a festival market on summer weekends. Its two-story Head House, added in 1803 for meetings and storage of fire equipment, is now an easy landmark for people to find on their way to South Street.

There is no synagogue in sight in this 1859 photograph. Instead, the Spruce Street Baptist Church dominates the view. It was originally built in 1829, in simple Federal style, by a young member of the Baptist congregation, Thomas U. Walter; it was his first architectural project. After gaining fame for his completion of the U.S. Capitol building, Walter returned in 1851 and gave the church a Classical Revival appearance, adding distinctive twin cupolas.

By the dawn of the twentieth century, the Baptist congregation dwindled while the neighborhood had become a haven for Jewish immigrants. In 1910, the building took on a new life, with the Yiddish carving over the front door "Great Roumanian Synagogue." Saved from demolition as the area turned upscale, it is now the thriving Society Hill Synagogue.

The last person to be officially hanged in the area that is now called Logan Circle was William Gross, in 1823. This was one of five squares that William Penn had planned as city parks. It served not only as an execution grounds but as a graveyard and pasture for local cows and horses. In 1825, it was named for James Logan, Penn's secretary. Only after the new parkway was paved from City Hall to the art museum did it become a traffic circle.

The Swann Memorial Fountain was completed in 1924 by Alexander Sterling Calder. This member of the famed Calder family is the "middleman" on the parkway. His work is situated midway between his father's 250 monumental sculptures on City Hall and a mobile created by his famous son, Alexander Calder, that hangs in the Philadelphia Museum of Art. The Swann fountain features three graceful allegorical figures representing the Delaware, Schuylkill, and Wissahickon rivers. New skyscrapers dominate the background of the photo.

The Grand Lodge of Free and Accepted Masons of Pennsylvania was established in 1727, the first masonic lodge in the American colonies. Its members included many of the nation's founders; George Washington's masonic apron, which he wore to lay the cornerstone of the U.S. Capitol building in 1793, is on exhibit in the museum. This 1868 photograph shows the northeast corner of Broad and Filbert streets prior to the construction of the Masonic Temple.

As the Masons prospered in the city, they erected ever grander
temples, culminating at last in the extraordinary Norman-style Grand
Lodge, now occupying the corner of Broad and Filbert. Each of the
seven magnificent lodge halls inside is designed in a different period
style. Egyptian Hall, complete with authentic hieroglyphics, is the
most famous. Free tours of the building are offered regularly.

In 1795, Charles Willson Peale lined the second floor of Independence Hall with paintings—the results of the art education program he had started in 1791 and the forerunner of America's first art museum, organized in 1805. The museum's fourth and current building is Frank Furness's Victorian Gothic masterpiece on Broad Street. In 1876, he fused a riot of brownstone, red and black bricks, purple terra-cotta, squat stone columns like pistons, and exotic sandstone carvings of birds and flowers into a single design.

The curriculum of the Pennsylvania Academy of the Fine Arts featured figure classes with lectures from both artists and leading physicians. The renowned artist Thomas Eakins, formerly an Academy student, became director in 1882, but was dismissed for insisting that female art students be permitted to sketch nude male models. Distinguished alumni include Maxfield Parrish, Mary Cassatt, John Sloan, architect Louis I. Kahn, and movie director David Lynch.

"Whatever was dingy, coarse, and ugly, is transformed. The streets, bathed in the fresh morning light, fairly sparkle . . . a new city for a new day." Inspired by Paris, Charles Mulford Robinson was advancing the "City Beautiful" movement that swept through America's older industrial cities. This 1909 photograph from City Hall's tower shows crowded buildings gray with soot from the factories and the railroad. The tower of the Pennsylvania Railroad Terminal, the world's largest, can be seen in the foreground.

Eight years and hundreds of demolished buildings later, Philadelphia paved its grand boulevard from Fairmount Park to City Hall. It was soon lined with buildings such as the Philadelphia Free Library and the Franklin Institute. In the center of this recent photograph is the Philadelphia Museum of Art on the hill at the northwest end of the city's "Champs-Élysées," with modern buildings beginning to crowd the vista.

The new Franklin Institute and Museum had just been built when this early photograph was taken in April 1934. Before the final wall of the building was enclosed in 1933, the 101-foot-long Baldwin 60000, the largest steam locomotive ever made, was pulled on temporary tracks to its place of honor in the institute. Philadelphia's Baldwin Company was then in decline as diesel engines replaced steam. Because of a transportation strike, this proud 350-ton machine had to be inched along to its destination by teams of horses.

Originally founded in 1824 to celebrate Benjamin Franklin and his scientific accomplishments, the Franklin Institute established the nation's first weather bureau and the first formal courses in architecture. Visitors to today's Franklin Institute on the Benjamin Franklin Parkway can still ride the locomotive or experiment with electricity and other scientific advances. On their way to the IMAX theater, they can climb through a two-story human heart.

Philadelphia's Rodin Museum has the only collection of sculptures by Auguste Rodin to rival his Paris museum. Theater magnate Jules E. Mastbaum began collecting Rodin's works in 1923, and planned for the building that would make them available to the public. He commissioned French architects Jacques Greber and Paul Cret to design the museum and garden on the Benjamin Franklin Parkway.

The Rodin Museum features two versions of his most famous work. *The Thinker* appeared first as a relatively small statue at the pinnacle of his grand tragic frieze, *The Gates of Hell*. Later, he completed a much larger cast, now at the parkway entrance to the museum. *The Burghers* *of Calais*, *Eternal Springtime*, and *The Apotheosis of Victor Hugo* are among the museum's 124 holdings. The Rodin Museum is open to the public for a nominal fee.

At the time of its completion in 1928, the Philadelphia Museum of Art was the largest Classical Revival building in the world. One critic referred to it as "that great Greek garage." Although Horace Trumbauer is usually credited with the design, architectural historians have begun to recognize the museum as more the work of his chief designer, the African American architect Julian Abele. After having just visited Greece, he had originally proposed three separate Greek temples for the site.

In addition to one of the finest collections of art in America, the museum contains a fantastic stone staircase (*above*) and is surrounded by dozens of extraordinary sculptures. One of the most unique is a bronze *Charioteer of Delphi*, cast from the original in Athens. It is a gift from the Greek government: "From the Cradle of Democracy in the Old World to the Cradle of Democracy in the New." In the foreground of both photographs is one of the great heroic monuments to George Washington.

Stealing a twenty-dollar watch brought Charles Williams the dubious honor of being the first prisoner at Eastern State Penitentiary. The world's first penitentiary began as a Quaker-inspired experiment to see if a prisoner would eventually repent if given enough time to meditate in solitude. The cheerless fortress walls were intended to impress upon the public the "misery which awaits the unhappy being who enters." Inside the thirty-foot walls, John Haviland had designed America's first radial prison with cell blocks radiating from a central hub.

Pennsylvania governor Gifford Pinchot sentenced his black lab, Pep, to life in the pen for killing the family's pet cat in 1924. Pep's six years as a mascot at Eastern State Penitentiary earned him a place on a long list of celebrity inmates, including Willie Sutton and Al Capone. Capone actually hosted the warden for dinner in his luxury cell. Eastern State Penitentiary is now a popular tourist attraction.

Left: This 1876 photograph catches the edge of the Schuylkill River where the Spring Garden Bridge is crossing to the Centennial fairgrounds and the steamboats are preparing to cruise up the river. Above the waterworks, the enormous reservoir on "Fair Mount Hill" is providing fresh water to the city. Church steeples and smokestacks are the tallest structures in the skyline. Philadelphia's City Hall tower has not yet been built.

Right: This recent photograph shows the pivotal place of the Philadelphia Museum of Art. Replacing the reservoir on Fairmount Hill, it stands at the head of the parkway, slicing diagonally through William Penn's chessboard street plan to Center City. The museum also anchors the roads and pathways that wind north along the Schuylkill through Fairmount Park. The modern skyline now dwarfs the steeples of an earlier century.

Left: Philadelphia City Hall, the world's largest stack of bricks (88 million), has been admired and denounced for a century. Poet Walt Whitman called it "silent, weird, beautiful." Others called it an appalling "marble elephant" and pressed to demolish it. With walls 27 feet thick and 650 feet long, the 651-room building is the world's largest masonry building. It is also America's finest example of French Second Empire architecture. The inset shows the scale of the William Penn statue, which is located on the top of the tower.

Above: Over 250 sculptures by Alexander Milne Calder adorn City Hall. *Repentance* and *Pain* loom over the prisoners' entrance while stone cats frolic with stone mice at another entrance. The tower is crowned by the largest statue on a building in the world, the 37-foot-tall statue of William Penn (*see inset*). After the highly detailed statue was completed in the studio, it was dismantled and each of the fourteen pieces was hoisted to the top of the tower.

In 1851, a serene corner on Broad Street became the site for "Operas in English and Italian, concerts, drama, pantomime and French Vaudeville." Architect Napoleon Le Brun left the exterior "perfectly plain and simple" and spent the funds on the interior. To achieve the best acoustics, his engineers tried to create a dancing column of air by constructing a thirty-foot concave dome in the ceiling opposite a thirty-foot brick well in the basement. The floorboards were laid to vibrate like a sounding board.

The American premiere of Verdi's *Il Trovatore* opened the Academy of Music's first season in 1857. Subsequent academy premieres included Gounod's *Faust*, Strauss's *Ariadne auf Naxos*, and Wagner's *The Flying Dutchman*. The academy also hosted circus acts and the world's first indoor football game in 1889 when planks were spread over the orchestra seats. Today, America's oldest opera house boasts rich ceiling murals and red velvet seats, crowned by a 5,000-pound crystal chandelier (*see inset*).

This 1920s view up South Broad Street is dominated by one of Philadelphia's first skyscrapers, the Atlantic Building. The Academy of Music, with a wide awning, can be seen farther up the street. But it is the twenty-first-century replacement for the building at lower left that has caught Philadelphia's imagination—the dramatic new Kimmel Center for the Performing Arts.

As with the Academy of Music up the street, unique measures were taken to ensure the best sound quality in the Kimmel Center. Its two performing spaces "float" on blocks of rubber to limit vibrations and noise from the subway and the surrounding city. Internationally renowned architect Rafael Vinoly took the classical arch from Philadelphia's architectural psyche and expanded it into a great glass vault over the building (*above*). As Vinoly explained, "You have to make a landmark for a city of monuments."

Left: This 1940s photo is a view of Market Street looking west from the City Hall plaza. Modest commercial enterprises on the left side face the remnants of the Pennsylvania Railroad Station on their way to demolition. The world's largest train station dominated this side of downtown Philadelphia (*see inset*). Steam locomotives from New York, Chicago, and Washington would reach the Schuylkill River, turn around, and head back into Center City Philadelphia, belching soot on the urban landscape.

Above: Removal of the station and its "Chinese Wall" of tracks freed up the area west of City Hall for full commercial development. Once Liberty One broke the code and became the tallest structure in Philadelphia, it attracted other modern skyscrapers. Now Market Street West is the most exciting commercial section of Center City Philadelphia. Claes Oldenburg's famous clothespin sculpture rises from a subway entrance on the left side of the photo. Philadelphia has more public art than any other city in the world.

Holy Trinity Church, built in 1859 on Rittenhouse Square, is in true Romanesque design—a fortress of brownstone. It was here in 1868 that the church organist first played the gentle Christmas carol "O Little Town of Bethlehem," written by pastor Phillips Brooks. Philadelphia's most upscale neighborhood for 150 years, Rittenhouse Square was ringed by Victorian mansions for the city's rich and famous: Wanamaker, Wharton, Biddle, and Curtis. The world-renowned Curtis Institute of Music is located just off the square.

William Penn had designated the square as one of five open parks when he first planned his capital city in 1681. High-rise condos and Victorian mansions, trendy shops, and gourmet restaurants combine with the square's lush landscaping to make Rittenhouse Square one of America's most desirable neighborhoods. In this photograph, Holy Trinity Church is complemented by a modern building, the Rittenhouse. Architect Donald Reiff positioned this hotel/condominium at an angle to permit unobstructed views of the square. Both photographs were taken from the rooftop terrace of the Claridge Apartments.

The Philadelphia Waterworks was a top tourist destination in the nineteenth century. Paved courts, canals, gardens, walkways, and handsome Roman temples provided a grand promenade for the thousands who came to see one of the great accomplishments of the new industrial age. A groundbreaking feat of engineering, a turbine system pumped four million gallons of water each day up to an enormous reservoir on "Fair Mount," then dispersed it by a gravity system throughout Philadelphia.

The great engineer Frederick Graff was the first to plan a system of fire hydrants and underground pipes to provide sanitary water for the poor and to help fight fires. Cities around the world subsequently adopted similar systems of hydrants. Architect Benjamin Latrobe designed a cluster of classical Roman temples to house the waterworks. The main Philadelphia Waterworks building has recently been restored as a romantic riverside restaurant.

At the bend where the Schuylkill choked with silt and became "too thick to drink, too thin to plow," boat sheds sprang up in the early 1800s. The dam built for the Philadelphia Waterworks had produced a calm surface upriver, creating one of the world's best waterways for rowing contests. By 1900, an elegant line of Victorian Gothic boathouses stretched along the bend. One of them, the Undine Barge Club, was designed by renowned architect Frank Furness.

The Schuylkill Navy, America's oldest amateur sports organization, was formed from ten clubs in 1858 to promote and regulate racing. The first women's association, the Sedgeley Club, took over the Skating and Humane Society building, which has a lighthouse used to warn boaters of the dam ahead. Each May the Dad Vail Regatta draws the top college rowing teams to America's largest championship meet. Special lights, originally meant just for the holidays, outline the boathouses every night—an act of whimsy that has become one of the city's most popular postcard pictures.

MOUNT PLEASANT

Among the dozens of eighteenth-century country houses that remain in Fairmount Park, Mount Pleasant is regarded as one of the finest Georgian homes in America. It was built in 1761 for Captain John MacPherson, a Scottish privateer. Like many of the country houses built along the Schuylkill River, Mount Pleasant was designed with two front doors—one facing the river and one facing the long drive from colonial Philadelphia.

The estate proved so costly that MacPherson was finally forced to sell it in 1779. One of George Washington's generals purchased it as a wedding present for his bride; but before Benedict Arnold and Peggy could move in, he was on the run for treason. This house is under the management of the Philadelphia Museum of Art and is open for tours.

Two hundred buildings in Fairmount Park hosted America's first successful world's fair to celebrate the nation's centennial in 1876. These included twenty-four Victorian buildings for the states, fifteen buildings for participating nations, and the colossal Main Exhibition building, over five football fields long and covering twenty-three acres. Memorial Hall, the central building of the fair, was actually designed by the park's engineer, and was so highly admired that Germany's parliament was modeled after it.

Over ten million people—a quarter of the U.S. population—attended the centennial celebrations. America's advances in technology were shown to the world: the telephone, the typewriter, and Hires Root Beer. With the Civil War's wounds still raw, the Centennial Exposition helped to heal the hurt nation. Memorial Hall served as Philadelphia's art museum until 1926, when the current Museum of Art opened. One of the few permanent buildings at the Centennial Exposition, Memorial Hall is used today for special events in the park.

JOHNSON HOUSE

Left: The Johnson House, in the Germantown section of Philadelphia, was part of the Underground Railroad, the network of houses that harbored fugitive slaves as they fled to freedom through Pennsylvania. As early as 1688, the German and Dutch settlers of Germantown had declared their opposition to "this traffik of men-body. Such men ought to be delivered out of ye hands . . . and set free." Their written protest stands as the earliest antislavery declaration in America.

Above: One of the best-preserved Underground Railroad sites, this 1768 building is a National Historic Landmark, now open for tours and special programs. Visitors are shown the special hiding places where the Johnson family stowed runaway slaves in the 1850s, until they could be moved through other Quaker villages to eventual freedom. The Johnsons also hosted meetings for abolitionist leaders William Still and Harriet Tubman in their home.

This mill town was originally called Flat Rock because of the nearby boulder-strewn Schuylkill River. Since the river served as a major means to transport goods to and from Philadelphia, the boat-wrecking boulders necessitated the construction of a canal to circumvent the danger. Consequently, the small town burgeoned from eight hundred to six thousand residents. Its gunpowder mills churned out most of the munitions used in the Civil War.

Flat Rock was renamed Manayunk after the Lenape word *manaiung*, which means "where we drink." Between the working-class neighborhood bars that remain on the side streets and the tony restaurants and microbreweries on the gentrified Main Street, Manayunk still lives up to its name as the place where people drink. The canal towpath has also taken on new life with cyclists and joggers.

Left: In this picture of the world's largest city park, the 1855 wood truss bridge is being replaced by a new Girard Avenue bridge on the Schuylkill. A 1695 stone cottage and dozens of eighteenth-century country homes are preserved among the 3,000 acres of Fairmount Park, marking the lives of the colonial settlers. Nineteenth-century notables can be found in Laurel Hill Cemetery, where rich families jostling for "a tomb with a view" occasionally built tombs too close to the edge—and they slipped over the side.

Above: Fairmount Park has something for everyone: America's oldest zoo; the Mann Music Center, summer home for the Philadelphia Orchestra; and miles of cycling and jogging trails, world-rated climbing cliffs, and bridle paths. Art lovers will discover hundreds of public sculptures, including Milles's *Playing Angels*, Lipchitz's *The Spirit of Enterprise*, and Remington's largest bronze *Cowboy*, a fascinating study in arrested motion.

America's pioneer botanist was the self-taught John Bartram, and the stone house he built with his own hands 250 years ago still stands on the west bank of the Schuylkill River. He explored the East Coast from Florida to Ontario, making notes on the people and wildlife and collecting specimens of plants for his farm. Bartram's correspondence with London Quaker Peter Collinson was the start of a burgeoning export business in seeds and plants.

John Bartram's house and garden are restored and open to the public. Visitors can follow in the footsteps of George Washington, Thomas Jefferson, and Samuel Powel, who all viewed Bartram's collection of rare plants and discussed his botanical experiments. They can also see an example of the unusual flowering tree *Franklinia altamaha*, which John Bartram named in honor of his friend and fellow experimenter, Ben Franklin.

INDEX

Abele, Julian 112
Abercrombie House 88, 89
Academy of Music 73, 120, 121, 122, 123
Adams, John 5, 17, 95
African American Museum 24, 25
Allen, Reverend Richard 56
Arch Street 25
Arch Street Friends Meetinghouse 22, 23
Asbury, Francis 9
Athenaeum 8 6, 87
Atlantic Building 122, 123
Baldwin Locomotive Works 5, 108
Bartram, John 142, 143
Benjamin Franklin Bridge 6, 7, 9, 29
Benjamin Franklin Parkway 42, 43, 101, 106, 107, 109, 110
Betsy Ross House 10, 11, 14
Biddle, Nicholas 59
Blodgett, Samuel 81
Boathouse Row 130, 131
Bonaparte House 76, 77
Bourse Building 62, 63
Bouvier, Michael 76
Broad Street 102, 103, 104, 121, 122, 123
Calder, Alexander Milne 119
Calder, Alexander Sterling 101
Capone, Al 115
Carpenters' Hall 54, 55, 84
Center City 7, 42, 43, 116, 117, 125
Chestnut Street 52
Chestnut Street Theater 5
Christ Church 5, 14, 40, 41
City Hall 5, 26, 42, 43, 106, 107, 116, 118, 119, 125
City Tavern 5, 17
Classical Revival 81, 98, 112
Clay Studio 14, 15

Collinson, Peter 142
Colonial Revival 53
Congress Hall 66, 67
Corn Exchange 52, 53
Cret, Paul 6, 110
Curtis Institute of Music 126
Delancey Houses 92, 93
Delaware River 18, 25, 30, 52, 74
Dolley Todd House 78, 79
Douglass, Frederick 57
Drinker, John 92
Duffield, George 64, 65
Eastern State Penitentiary 114, 115
Eighth Street 32
Elfreth's Alley 12, 13, 14
Fairmount Park 5, 107, 117, 132, 134, 140, 141
Fifth Street 40, 63
Filbert Street 102, 103
First Bank 80, 81
First National Bank 59
Fitch, John 5
Fourth and Prune 94, 95
Fourth Street 9, 29, 47, 79
Franklin, Benjamin 5, 24, 40, 41, 44, 46, 50, 54, 60, 61, 75, 76, 86, 109
Franklin Institute 107, 108, 109
Free Library 107
Front Street 16
Furness, Frank 39, 104, 130
Girard, Stephen 81
Girard Avenue Bridge 141
Graff, Frederick 129
Graff, Jacob 38
Graff House 38, 39
Greber, Jacques 110
Greek Revival 5, 69, 82
Gross, William 100
Hamilton, Alexander 80
Hamilton, Andrew 67
High Street 97
Hill, Henry 48

Holy Trinity Church 126, 127
Howe, George 26
Independence Hall (Pennsylvania Statehouse) 38, 45, 49, 67, 104
Italian Renaissance 20, 31
Jefferson, Thomas 5, 38, 39, 44, 61, 143
John Bartram's House and Garden 142, 143
Johnson House 136, 137
Kimmel Center 5, 122, 123
Latrobe, Benjamin 129
Laurel Hill Cemetery 141
Le Brun, Napoleon 28
Leiper, Thomas 5
Lemon Hill 116, 117
Lescaze, William 26
Library Company 60, 61
Lit Brothers Store 32, 33
Logan, James 100
Logan Circle Fountain 100, 101
London Coffee House 16, 17
MacPherson, John 132, 132
Madison, James 44, 79
Manayunk 138, 139
Market Street 16, 18, 19, 27, 32, 35, 38, 39, 124, 125
Masonic Temple 102, 103
Mastbaum, Jules E. 110
Memorial Hall 134, 135
Merchant's Exchange 82, 83
Morris, Robert 9
Mother Bethel Church 56, 57
Mott, Lucretia 23, 57
Mount Pleasant 132, 133
Mulberry Street 24, 25
Musical Fund Hall 72, 73
Newmarket 96, 97
Ninth Street 76
Old City 14, 15
Oldenburg, Claes 125
Olde St. Mary's Church 95

Old Pine Street Church 64, 65
Old Swedes Church 74, 75
Peale, Charles Willson 59, 84, 85, 104
Penn, William 5, 12, 18, 42, 43, 93, 100, 117, 119, 127
Pennsylvania Academy of the Fine Arts 104, 105
Pennsylvania Convention Center 31
Pennsylvania Hospital 50, 51
Pennsylvania Railroad Terminal 106, 125
Philadelphia Contributionship 46, 47
Philadelphia Museum of Art 42, 101, 107, 112, 113, 117, 133
Philadelphia Waterworks 5, 128, 129, 130
Philosophical Hall 44, 45
Physick, Dr. Philip Syng 48, 49, 51
Physick House 48, 49
Pine Street 64, 92
Poe, Edgar Allan 37
Poe House 36, 37
Powel, Samuel 90, 143
Powel House 90, 91
PSFS Building 26, 27
Quakers 13, 22, 71, 90, 114, 137, 142
Reading Terminal 30, 31
Reiff, Donald 127
Renaissance Revival 5, 32, 86
Richardson Romanesque 57
Rittenhouse, David 24, 25
Rittenhouse Square 126, 127
Robinson, Charles Mulford 106
Rodin Museum 110, 111
Rush, Benjamin 50
Rush, William 84

Schuylkill River 116, 117, 125, 130, 132, 138, 141, 142
Second Bank 58, 59
Second Street 52, 89
Seventh Street 24, 32, 37, 38
Shippen, Dr. William 94
Sixth Street 30
Smith, Robert 55, 84, 87
Smythe Building 20, 21
Society Hill 5, 64, 89, 91, 93, 97
Society Hill Synagogue 98, 99
South Street 70, 71
Spring Garden 37
Spring Garden Bridge 116
Spruce Street Baptist Church 98
St. Augustine's Church 28, 29
St. George's Church 8, 9
St. Peter's Church 84, 85
Strickland, William 59, 82, 84
Swann Memorial Fountain 101
Todd, John 79
Trumbauer, Horace 112
Twelfth Street 35
Walnut Street 79
Walnut Street Theatre 5, 68, 69
Walter, Thomas U. 46, 98
Wanamaker, John 35
Wanamaker Store 34, 35
Washington, George 5, 9, 13, 14, 17, 28, 40, 43, 66, 80, 85, 90, 95, 102, 113, 133, 143
Weisgerber, Charles 10, 11
Williams, Charles 114
Wistar, Caspar 94